The Rebirth of New York City's
Bryant Park

Front cover: Bryant Park, New York City
Photo by Frank Garnier, Olin Partnership

Publisher: James G. Trulove
Designer: Sarah Vance
Assistant Designer: Elizabeth Reifeiss
Editor: D. Sperry Finlayson
Production Coordinator: Susan McNally
Printer: Palace Press, Hong Kong

ISBN 1-888931-05-1

Contents

Acknowledgments

The restoration of Bryant Park would have been impossible without the financial aid, energy, intelligence, hard work, and perseverance of a great number of individuals and organizations. The citizens of New York are their beneficiaries.

The client was Bryant Park Restoration Corporation led throughout the duration of the project by Andrew Heiskell, Chairman, Daniel Biederman, President, and Lorna Nove, Executive Assistant. A prime catalyst for the project and the client for the restoration of the Fifth Avenue terrace portion of the park was the New York Public Library, whose complete revitalization was led by its President, Vartan Gregorian. Marshall Rose, the Library Board Chairman, like Heiskell a member of both boards, provided sage leadership throughout. Arthur Rosenblatt as project manager for the initial years assisted both organizations.

Lew Davis of Davis Brody Architects, led the entire renovation of the New York Public Library as well as the expansion and construction of the underground stacks beneath the park. Hugh Hardy of Hardy, Holzman, Pfeiffer was the architect for all of the kiosks and cafes created on the Fifth Avenue terrace and within the park. Koupic and Koutsomitis restored the public restrooms and maintenance structures.

William H. Whyte not only provided the key sociological study of behavior within the park, but also bold and effective programmatic and management strategies, as well as inspiring us with his clear moral vision and great love of life, New York, and humanity—in short, with his wisdom and wit.

Without good contractors capable of unusual and creative efforts, it would have been impossible. Tishman Construction Corporation was the construction manager. The general contractor was Lastrada General Contracting Corporation. Lewis and Valentine Nurseries, Inc. was the landscape contractor, and Pansini Stone Setting, Inc. was the masonry contractor.

Our consultants not only had the technical, artistic and coordination difficulties associated with a long complex urban project, but in several instances were instrumental in fund-raising for the construction costs of their work as well as their own fees and deserve our gratitude. Howard M. Brandston and Partners were the lighting designers. Joseph R. Loring was the civil, electrical and mechanical engineer. Robert R. Rosenwasser was the structural engineer. Lynden B. Miller executed the final design and installation of the perennial beds, located a gardener for BPRC and helped establish the maintenance and volunteers which have helped out since completion of the construction.

At Hanna/Olin Ltd. many people helped over a twelve year period. Alistair MacIntoch was the associate-in-charge in the design stages at the beginning, turning the reins over to Christopher N. Allen who supervised construction of the Fifth Avenue terrace and then supervised the entire remainder of the project, from final design through construction. Craig McGlynn, Elizabeth Meyer, and David Dougherty were at times project manager. Edgar David, Joseph Eades, Christine Eaton, Lucy Karlsson, Barry Kew, Barbara Merkel, and David Rieseck all worked on various aspects in design, documentation, and construction. Frank Garnier was responsible for graphics and reports and helped with various studies and publications including this one.

To everyone mentioned above, I offer my deepest appreciation and thanks for their help. Finally, I owe a debt of gratitude to my partners of this period, Robert M. Hanna and Dennis McGlade, and to my wife, Victoria Steiger, who sustained and supported me throughout this long and at times difficult and contentious project.

Laurie Olin
Olin Partnership
Philadelphia, 1997

The Rebirth of New York City's Bryant Park

by J. William Thompson

When Laurie Olin recounts the story of the restoration of New York's Bryant Park, he likes to show his audience an aerial photograph that looks straight down into the canyons of midtown Manhattan, which he calls "one of the highest-density places on the planet." Amid the imploding forest of skyscrapers in that photograph, Bryant Park is the only visible open space. "Thousands of people cooped up in rooms and corridors need places where they can change their depth of focus and be in nature while in the heart of the city," says Olin. The restored Bryant Park seems to provide just such a well-ordered breathing space for perennially stressed New Yorkers.

From seven o'clock in the morning, when early bench-sitters sip latte and cappuccino, available from an on-site kiosk, until closing time at 6:00 P.M. (9:00 in the summer), the new Bryant Park is one of the most-frequented spots in midtown. The park presents programmed activities almost every day: book readings and signings, outdoor concerts, and fashion shows. Vintage films, projected on an outdoor screen every Monday night during the summer, draw crowds of more than 2,000 people. Frequently referred to as midtown's "Town Square," the nine-acre park is a potent marketing tool for adjacent real estate; one year after its opening the *New York Times* reported that office leasing in the vicinity had increased significantly, and cited the restored park as the reason.[1]

But the restoration of Bryant Park is an important project for reasons that extend beyond midtown Manhattan. At a time when older urban centers are increasingly seen as dingy and dangerous, New York City's investment in Bryant Park is a gesture representing enormous optimism about the future of cities, and the public response to the restored park seems to validate that optimism. At a time of shrinking public park budgets, the fact that Bryant Park has been restored and maintained largely with private funds, together with an assessment levied on adjacent real estate, makes it a model for public/private partnerships in the cause of urban open space. Finally, Bryant Park's success is a testimony to the importance of careful design in the rehabilitation of historic landscapes; for the "new" Bryant Park must be understood as an adaptive reuse, not a literal restoration. It may look much like the historic park, but it invites very different uses and constituencies. It contains, moreover, at least one virtually invisible use that was never envisioned in the design of the original park: two levels of stacks, to house 3.2 million volumes of the New York Public Library's holdings, are concealed under the lush central lawn.

Bryant Park was a very different place in 1982 when, sketch book in hand, Laurie Olin walked through and around the park, drawing and taking notes. Olin, a partner in Philadelphia-based Hanna/Olin Ltd., had just been commissioned to undertake the park's redesign and restoration. He and his partner at the time, Robert Hanna, had earned a reputation for sensitivity to urban contexts, with work ranging from Westlake Park in downtown Seattle to the restoration of the grounds at the American Academy in Rome. Landscape architect Peter Walker once said of Hanna/ Olin's work, "It's so refined, it almost goes away." [2]

Tall, bearded, and urbane, Olin looks the part of an academic; and, in fact, at the time he accepted the Bryant Park commission he was also assuming the chairmanship of the Department of Landscape Architecture at the Harvard Graduate School of Design. But on that day in 1982 when he walked through the park, sketching, Olin was all practitioner. This was not

his first visit; he had lived in New York in the 1960s—had, in fact, witnessed a shooting in Bryant Park in 1968. By the eighties, conditions had deteriorated even further. "A sense of neglect pervades the place— pigeon shit and drugs," Olin jotted in his sketch book. It was drugs, of course, not pigeons, that posed the real problem—or, more specifically, the fact that the drug dealers had appropriated much of the park. Bryant Park had become the most flourishing outdoor drug market in New York City.

Urban designer Stephen Carr, who studied the park in the 1970s, caught the essence of this subculture in an unforgettable photograph to be found in his book, *Public Space*: a phalanx of young men is sitting or lounging shoulder to shoulder along the entire length of one of the park's balustrades. [3] Not surprisingly, the threatening presence of these drug dealers deterred many midtown office workers and residents from using the park at all. Muggings and other crimes generated media coverage that amplified the perception of risk. Most New Yorkers eventually shared the view that urban observer William Holly Whyte summed up very simply in his 1980 classic, *The Social Life of Small Urban Spaces*: "Bryant Park is dangerous." [4]

However, design, rather than sociology, was at the root of Bryant Park's problems. The park that Olin found in 1982 was designed according to the formerly widely held premise that urban parks should be refuges from the city. To this end, Bryant Park was physically removed from the surrounding streets by elevating it about four feet above street level and confining it within an iron fence. Entrances were few, narrow, and steep. Once inside, the visitor often found it impossible to reach a desired destination. "You got trapped by these dead ends," recalls Olin today. There were limestone balustrades that ran the length of the park—"300 linear feet with nowhere to go" in Olin's phrase. Finally, dense, overgrown shrubs blocked views into the park. Olin wrote, "It seems that the terraces and balustrades, the railings and plantings, which were meant to make life more gracious, have made it sinister. They allow for private turf to develop in a public place—an 'us and them' phenomenon. The park isn't open, accessible, one public place, but rather levels, cul-de-sacs, etc., removed from immediate and uniform access, surveillance, and social contact."

Similarly, Olin found evidence of public abandonment in the maintenance of the park. "Trees overgrown—ground beaten bare—trash overflowing the waste cans, stuffed into the long-abandoned light boxes—lights broken off and missing—pavement not repaired—hedges, allowed to grow up to hide the ugly lights, themselves look neglected and ugly," Olin noted in his sketch book. His overall verdict: "Ugly breeds ugly." As he walked around, Olin noticed, next to a monument to Andrade, a South American patriot, a group of drug users on the point of passing out. Others skulked off into the overgrown hedges. Those hedges, he found himself wondering— were people living in there? Would anyone want to go into this park, especially as dusk was falling?

The scene that Olin sketched in 1982 may have been Bryant Park at its historic nadir. But the park had never been the tranquil oasis it was intended to be. It had, rather, a history of intermittent social problems which culminated in a steady decline from the 1960s onward.

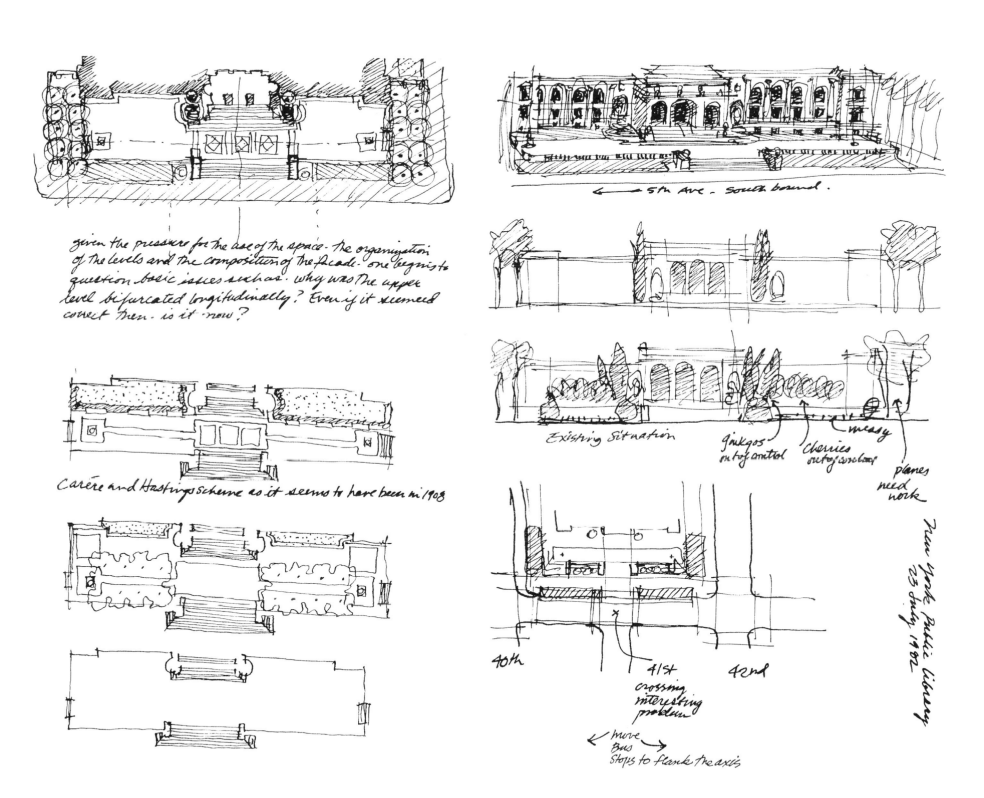

given the pressures for the use of the space. the organization
of the levels and the composition of the facade. one begins to
question basic issues such as. why was the upper
level bifurcated longitudinally? Even if it seemed
correct then. is it now?

Carère and Hastings scheme as it seems to have been in 1908

5th Ave. south bound.

Existing Situation

ginkgos
out of control

cherries
out of window

messy

planes
need
work

New York Public Library
23 July 1982

40th   41st   42nd

crossing
interesting
problem

← move →
Bus
Stops to flank the axis

*Notes from Laurie Olin's sketchbook of
conditions on Fifth Avenue terrace*

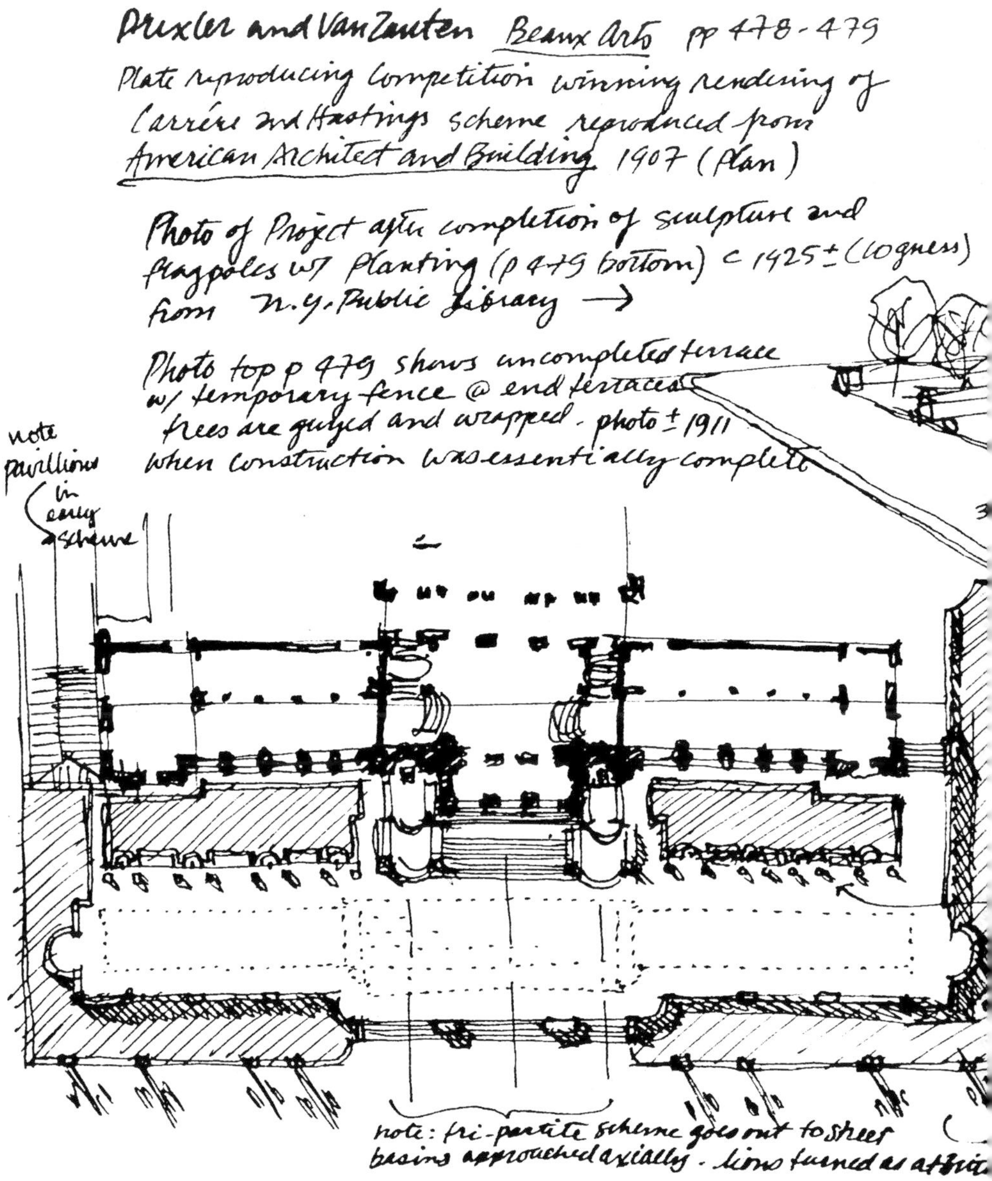

Drexler and VanZanten _Beaux Arts_ pp 478-479
Plate reproducing competition winning rendering of
Carrère and Hastings scheme reproduced from
American Architect and Building 1907 (Plan)

Photo of Project after completion of sculpture and
flagpoles w/ Planting (p 479 bottom) c 1925± (1 oguess)
from N.Y. Public Library →

Photo top p 479 shows uncompleted terrace
w/ temporary fence @ end terraces
trees are guyed and wrapped. photo ± 1911
when construction was essentially complete

note
pavillions
in
early
scheme

note: tri-partite scheme goes out to street
basins approached axially. lions turned as at front

Excerpt from Laurie Olin's initial research
on evolution of New York Public Library
environs

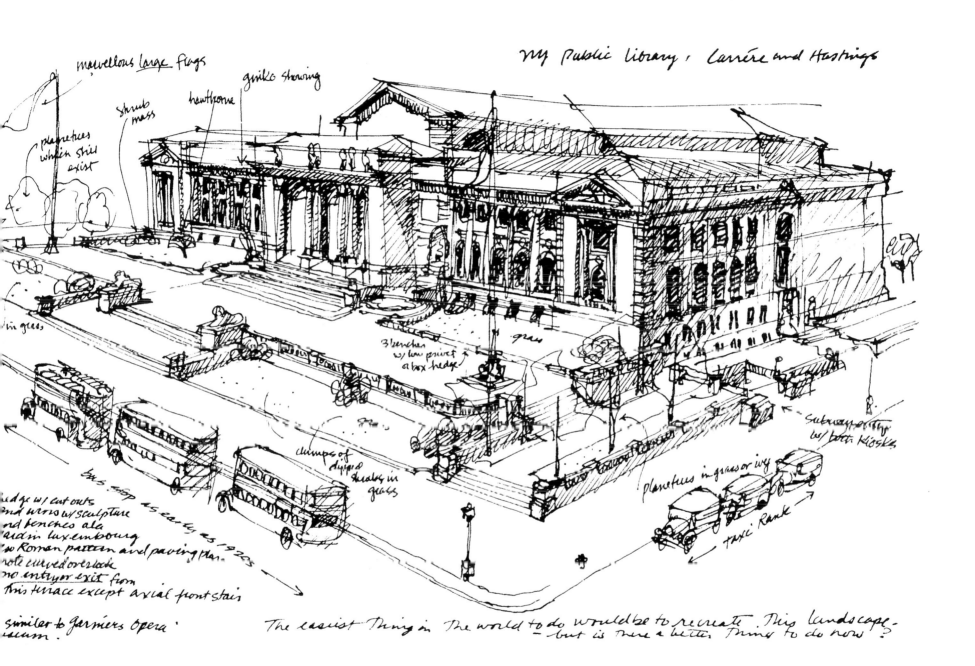

marvellous large flags

NY Public Library. Carrère and Hastings

ginkko showing

hawthorne

shrub mass

planetrees which still exist

in grass

3 benches w/ low privet or box hedge

grass

planetrees

subway entry w/ book kiosks

clumps of clipped shrubs in grass

bus stop as early as 1920s

edge w/ cut outs and urns w/ sculpture and benches ala Jardin Luxembourg so Roman pattern and paving plan.
note curved overlook
no entry or exit from this terrace except axial front stairs

similar to Garniers Opera Museum.

planetrees in grass or ivy

taxi Rank

The easiest thing in the world to do would be to recreate this landscape. — but is there a better thing to do now?

11

Problems:

Hey Baby!

Like man wow

← Trees overgrown - Ground beaten bare - trash overflow the waste cans - Stuffed into the long abandoned light boxes. Lights broken off and missing - pavement not repaired - hedges let to grow up to hide ugly lights, the well look neglected and ugly ugly breeds ugly -

↑ general population - fearful - mostly white, believing they are harassed, stressed overworked and preyed upon - apprehensive whities - look up and see terrace filled w/ blacks

giving each other high fives, smoking marijuana at all hours, buying, selling offering drugs to any passersby, while grooving and lazing about the whole place - full of trash

A sense of neglect pervades the place - Pigeon shit and drugs.

Scary past - below

hang about - above

Q: What to do?

- A: Break it down —— open it up.

The Stereotype and common perception

It seems that the terraces and balustrades, the railings and plantings which were meant to make life more gracious and somehow European, even mediterranean, have made it sinister - They allow for Private Turf to develope in a Public place - an us and them phenomena - it isn't open, accessable - one public place - but petty - levels, cul-de-sacs, etc. removed from immediate and uniform access - surveillance, and social contract which even a horn and hardarts or a Nedicks has - or the sidewalks.

Notes from Laurie Olin's sketchbook

we are at a moment in history where a little
more experiment might be in order.

ex.A: What if the walkway has a double
row of trees to give the passerbya
special place. but there is nothing
between this walk and the building
except an inner row of trees at the
sidewalk w/ flights of steps up to
the building?

B. eliminate inner row of trees etc.

C. etc.

As the environment becomes more impoverished
and inhospitable it also looks like it may be
safer.   Riddle -   What should we give up
— for what? . in terms of amenity —: color, texture,
movement, richness of materials, levels, forms, — for
another amenity —   The feeling of safety? When
physical comfort — shade, seating, etc... are also involved
in each shade off?

One hypothesis would be that the simplest thing to do to make this place work is to take
down the walls and railings. eliminate shrubs. ground covers, lawns, and flowers
— pave it all. have lots of stairs and ramps and walls to sit on.. even some
trees to provide shade in Bosque form. prob. locusts.

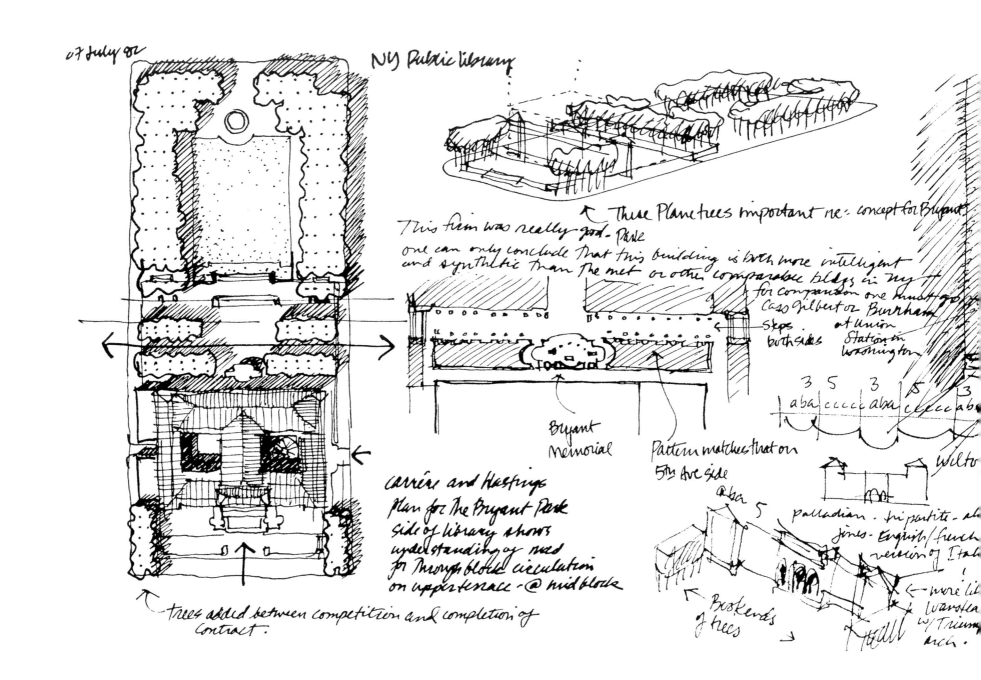

07 July 82

NY Public Library

↖ These Plane trees important re-concept for Bryant Park

This firm was really good - Park

one can only conclude that this building is both more intelligent and synthetic than the met or other comparable bldgs in ny

for comparison one must go Cass Gilbert or Burnham at Union Station in Washington

Steps both sides

3 5 3 5 3
aba ccccc aba ccccc aba

Bryant Memorial

Pattern matches that on 5th Ave side

Wilto

Carrère and Hastings plan for the Bryant Park side of library shows understanding of need for through block circulation on upper terrace - @ mid block

palladian - tripartite - al Jones - English / French version of Ital

↖ more lik Wansea w/ Trium arch

← Bookends of trees

← trees added between competition and completion of contract.

Observations entered into Laurie Olin's sketchbook of Bryant Park and library environs at beginning of project

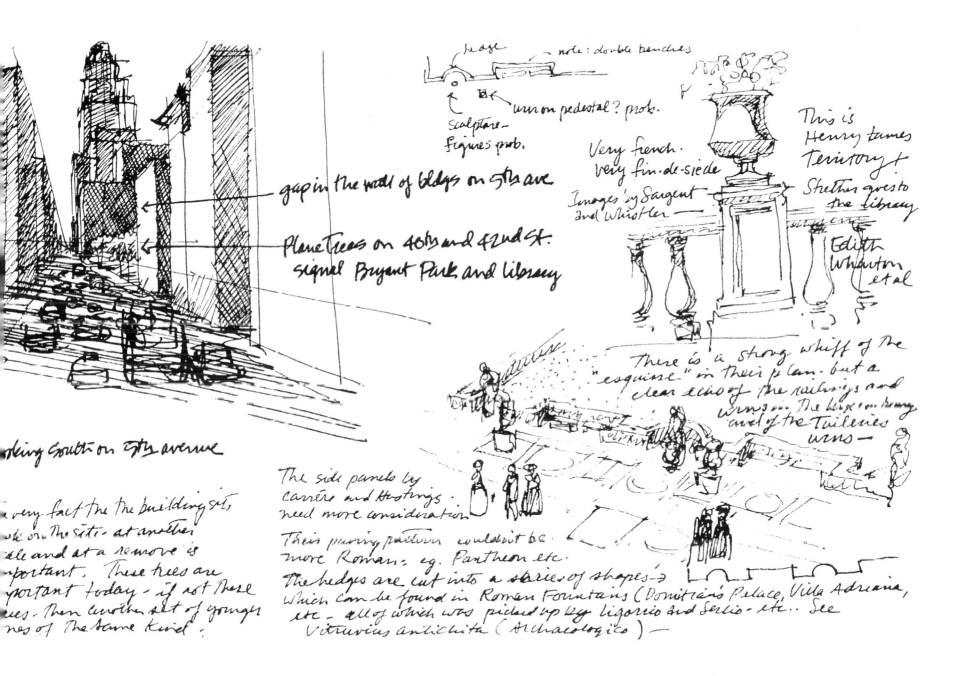

hedge — note: double benches

urn on pedestal? prob.

sculpture — figures prob.

gap in the wall of bldgs on 5th ave

Plane Trees on 40th and 42nd St. signal Bryant Park and library

Very french. very fin-de-siecle

Images by Sargent and Whistler —

This is Henry James Territory! Strether goes to the library

Edith Wharton et al

looking South on 5th avenue

In very fact the the building sits on the site - at another scale and at a remove is important. These trees are important today - if not these trees - then another set of younger ones of the same kind.

The side panels by Carrère and Hastings need more consideration

Their paving pattern couldn't be more Roman: eg. Pantheon etc.

The hedges are cut into a series of shapes → which can be found in Roman Fountains (Domitian's Palace, Villa Adriana, etc — all of which was picked up by Ligorio and Serlio - etc.. See Vitruvius antichità (Archaeologico) —

There is a strong whiff of the "esquisse" in their plan. but a clear echo of the railings and urns in the helix on bonny and of the Tuileries urns —

15

Bryant Park 24 July 83

*Sketch by Laurie Olin of Charles Adams
Platt's Lowell fountain and existing space
during early phase of commission*

The Egyptian revival style Croton Reservoir looking south from Fifth Avenue and 42nd Street

Crystal Palace exhibition building on the site of Bryant Park built for the U.S. Centennial celebration of 1876

Background:
The Gathering Clouds

The site of Bryant Park has a history of public use that dates back at least to 1839, the year the Croton Reservoir was built on what was then the periphery of New York City. The reservoir's walls, fifty feet high and thirty feet thick, allowed it a holding capacity of 21 million gallons. The top of the walls provided a place for an elevated promenade that became a fashionable spot for Sunday strolls (the site's earliest park-like use, as Olin likes to point out). The land adjacent to the reservoir—eventually Bryant Park—was designated a public park in 1846, and known as Reservoir Square, but it was not immediately developed as a park.

In 1853 a spectacular, iron and glass Crystal Palace-like pavilion was constructed on the site, to house the Exhibition of the Industry of All Nations. Five years later, the pavilion burned to the ground in fifteen minutes. During the Civil War, the space was used for the training of Union soldiers, seriously compromising any scenic qualities it may have possessed. Circular paths lined with benches and statuary were finally laid out

in 1871. In 1884, the site was renamed "Bryant Park" in honor of poet William Cullen Bryant, who, beginning in the 1840s, had used his position as editor of the *New York Times* to lead the movement to create Central Park.

In 1897 the Croton Reservoir was torn down to make way for the construction of the New York Public Library. The magnificent building, designed by the New York architecture firm of John M. Carrere and Thomas Hastings, opened in 1911. It enriched Bryant Park with a terrace behind the library, on which a bronze statue of Bryant by sculptor Herbert Adams sat in a massive chair within a marble niche. Two elaborate stone pavilions, housing men's and women's restrooms, stood at either end of the terrace. In 1912 the Lowell Memorial Fountain was added, in memory of Josephine Shaw Lowell, a pioneer social worker and suffragette.

From the beginning, Bryant Park seems to have suffered from a lack of maintenance, a condition aggravated by its use as a dumping ground during the construction of the Sixth Avenue subway. In 1921 jobless men camped out in the park. On January 23, 1928, the *New York*

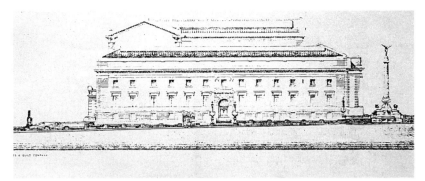

Carrere and Hastings winning scheme for Library design competition, 42nd Street facade elevation

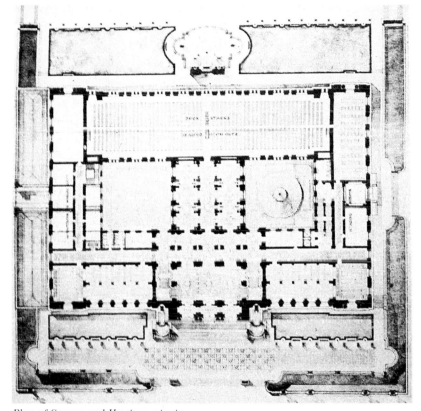

Plan of Carrere and Hastings winning scheme. The Fifth Avenue entry is at the bottom of the drawing and the rear terrace with the Bryant memorial is at the top

Times reported that Bryant Park had been for years a disgrace to the city. "Even before it was ruined by the subway excavation it was in dilapidated condition. Poorly planned, it had been inadequately maintained. Misused by the public, it was unsightly. No other city in the world would have tolerated such a park in one of the most important districts."[5] Conditions grew even worse after the stock market crash of 1929, when the park was abandoned to weeds and dereliction.

During the 1920s and early 1930s, more than a hundred plans for the rehabilitation of Bryant Park were proposed. (One prescient scheme called for a park that would be entirely open to the view of passersby on adjacent sidewalks; all walls, fences, and memorial statues that blocked sight lines would be eliminated.) It seems likely that among these hundred plans there were designs that would have proved more suitable than the one that was finally endorsed by powerful parks commissioner Robert Moses in the Depression year 1934. Lusby Simpson, an unemployed architect from Queens, had won first prize in a competition held by the Architects Emergency Employment Committee. His French Beaux-Art design was reminiscent of the Tuileries and the Jardins de Luxembourg, but called for ivy under the trees where the French might have used gravel, and for benches instead of the moveable chairs typically found in French parks. Simpson's plan proposed raising the park four feet above the level of surrounding sidewalks, planting 240 London plane trees along four paths flanking a large sunken lawn, and moving the park's fountain to a position near the Sixth Avenue entrance. Benches were to be set out along the bluestone walkways. Although its design intent—to create a restful sanctuary removed from the city—would prove to contain the seeds of future problems, Simpson's design was built. (One historical irony, discovered by the Hanna/Olin team in researching the history of the site: Moses invited his friend, landscape architect Gilmore Clark, to help implement the design, and Clark subsequently garnered a design award from the American Society of Landscape Architects for what was in fact Simpson's work.)

The park soon provided a venue for illicit activities. Arrests for loitering began in 1936, and in 1944 mayor Fiorello LaGuardia ordered a 10:00 P.M. curfew there. But it was not until the 1960s, and

View of the rear elevation of library shortly after completion showing the transitional modern wall of the stacks

Front facade and entry of the library around 1920

New Yorkers browsing through books in an outdoor reading room established in the rebuilt Bryant Park during the Great Depression

Bryant Park, not yet complete—note the planting pits awaiting their trees on the Sixth Avenue entry terrace—as a result of Robert Moses' initiative to rebuild it, 1935

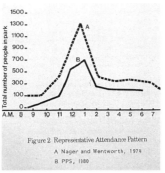

Figure 2. Representative Attendance Pattern
A Nager and Wentworth, 1974
B PPS, 1980

Decline in use documented by
William H. Whyte, 1980

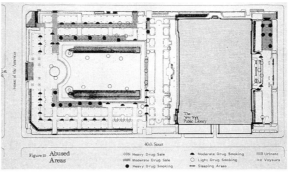

Figure 10 Abused Areas

Distribution of criminal and antisocial
activities in park as documented by
William H. Whyte, 1980

the urban social decay aggravated by the rise of the drug culture, that the defects inherent in Lusby Simpson's design mushroomed to truly malignant proportions. In 1966 a *New York Times* article labeled the park "a disaster area," a place attractive to "addicts, prostitutes, winos, and derelicts."[6] In an attempt to stop the park's deterioration, the Parks Department began scheduling free entertainment—dance, outdoor fashion shows, and poetry readings—there. For the first time, a parks commissioner proposed building a restaurant on the terrace behind the library, to attract mainstream users to the park. In spite of all such efforts—which, admittedly, were piecemeal and somewhat sporadic—Bryant Park became even more dangerous in the 1970s. In 1973 a parks commissioner threatened to close it unless the department somehow persuaded citizens to help with maintenance; in that same year wooden police barricades were installed across the park's entrances at 9:00 P.M., and periodic nightly patrols were instituted.

In 1974 Bryant Park was designated a New York City Landmark, even as muggings and marijuana dealing continued to escalate. It was, after all, a major public space in midtown Manhattan, and adjacent to a building of undoubted historical importance. In 1976 the first murder occurred in the park, and the idea of closing it down was proposed again, this time by the chairman of the local community board (which had influence with the city in matters of park management, if only in an advisory capacity). A second murder occurred in 1977. A proposal was put forth for the building of a tall iron boundary fence, to create a "library park" to which only the holders of library cards would be allowed access.

Not surprisingly, park attendance declined steadily during these years. A 1974 survey showed peak lunch-hour attendance at 1,300; by 1980, another study found only 700. Even more telling was the fluctuation in use over the course of a day—there was a "spike" of attendance during the lunch hour, followed by a virtual evacuation by mainstream users from 2:00 P.M. on. Another critical indicator of perceived security was the percentage of park users who were women: in the

1980 survey it rose from a woeful zero percent at 8:00 A.M. to a high of only 22 percent at midday.[7]

1979 was, however, the watershed year that would ultimately mark the beginning of the park's rebirth. In that year the New York Public Library embarked on a multimillion-dollar building renovation. Chairman Andrew Heiskell was advised by William Dietel, president of the Rockefeller Brothers Fund (headquartered in the neighborhood, and with direct, immediate knowledge of the park), that the library's "backyard" must be renewed as well. The library and the fund turned for guidance to respected urban analyst William H. (Holly) Whyte. His thirteen-page report to them begins:

> Bryant Park is now dominated by dope dealers, but they are not the cause of the problem. The basic problem is under-use. It has been for a long time. It antedated the invasion of the dope dealers and in part induced it. Access is the nub of the solution.[8]

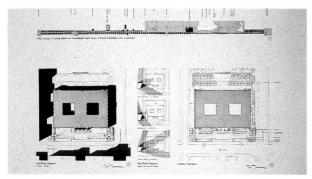

Hanna/Olin analysis of sun/shade and existing elements along Fifth Avenue and library entry terrace, 1980

The Way Back: A Process of Design

Many of those who have been intimately involved with Bryant Park's restoration regard it as a monument to the vision of Holly Whyte. Marshall Rose, director of the library, calls Whyte "one of our resident urban geniuses," and architectural critic Paul Goldberger said that he was "the true guiding light of this park . . . our prophet of urban space."[9] For Laurie Olin, Whyte is quite simply "our patron saint. . . .We tried to give physical form to some of his ideas."

Whyte, the author of *The Organization Man*, *The Last Landscape* and other books, is also a conservationist who, in the 1960s, became interested in the quality of the urban environment. (A lifelong city-dweller, he still lives on Manhattan's West Side.) In 1970, he formed the Street Life Project, a small research group intended to study the effects of crowding on central-city open spaces. When Whyte and his team ventured out into the streets, parks, and playgrounds of New York and began documenting what they saw, they found that many spaces—some of the plazas in front of corporate office buildings, for example—far

from being too crowded, were almost empty. As a result, they were often taken over by what Whyte generically called "undesirables," homeless persons and drug pushers. His team also found that in many of the most crowded streets and squares people did not seem to be suffering any of the supposed effects of overcrowding, but were behaving in a most sociable and convivial way. Whyte went on to develop a series of hypotheses about what made the good spaces work as well as they did, and these he developed into the recommendations for design and management that finally appeared, in 1980, in *The Social Life of Small Urban Spaces*. Whyte's research findings had transformed him into an effective spokesman for the civic use of the public realm.

It was natural, therefore, that the Rockefeller Brothers Fund would turn to Whyte for an analysis of the failure of Bryant Park. Whyte's central thesis, simple and convincing, was that the solution to the park's problems would be to promote its widest possible use by the public. He noted that if one were to apply his research findings in reverse, and strive to create a park that would be little used, one would elevate

Overgrown hedges and shaggy lawn, 1982

Group of addicts on rear terrace, 1982

Dappled light on mid-day lunch crowd, 1982

Forbidding entry from Sixth and 42nd Street intersection, 1982

it four feet above street level, put a wall around it, put a spiked iron fence atop the wall, and line the fence with thick shrubbery—exactly the conditions that existed at Bryant Park. To change them Whyte proposed the following:

Remove the iron fences

Remove the shrubbery

Cut openings in the balustrades for easier pedestrian circulation in and out of the park

Improve visual access up the steps on the Avenue of the Americas

Provide a third set of steps ("broad, and of an easy pitch") midway between the existing stairs on 42nd Street

Provide ramps for the handicapped

Open up access to the terrace at the back of the library with new steps

Restore the fountain

Rehabilitate Carrere and Hastings' historic restroom structures [10]

Note how conservative was the surgery that Whyte proposed for the restoration of the social functioning of Bryant Park. As Andrew Manshell, the Bryant Park Restoration Corporation's director of public amenities, said recently, "These are not grand ideas written on the landscape. Holly Whyte's not about big ideas. These are series of small landscape moves." However, Whyte's seemingly simple but carefully considered interventions, once implemented, were to prove enormously effective.

In 1980 the library and the Rockefeller Brothers Fund moved to implement Whyte's recommendations by forming the Bryant Park Restoration Corporation (BPRC), with the aid of the mayor, Abe Beam, and the parks commissioner, Gordon Davis. Daniel Biederman, a systems consultant and admirer of the ideas of Holly Whyte, was hired as executive director to launch a master plan. His strategy: to attack all the park's problems simultaneously rather than piecemeal, as had been tried previously; and to use the "carrot" (park improvements) more than the "stick" (police presence). [11]

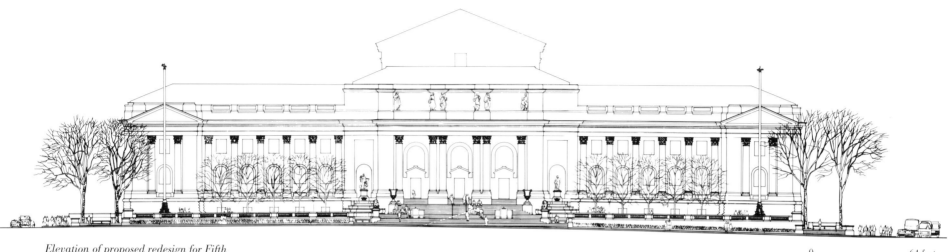

Elevation of proposed redesign for Fifth Avenue Terrace (Olin Partnership)

0   64 feet

Enormous blue construction fence acting as a billboard to announce changes and as a means to interrupt drug sales, erected long before construction actually occurred, 1980-1981

"Temporary" kiosk on Fifth Avenue terrace (by Hardy, Holzman, Pfeiffer), 1983

As plans for the rehabilitation of the park got underway, changes were afoot in front of the library as well. Lew Brody of Davis Brody Associates, architects to the library, had invited Hanna/Olin to redesign the terrace in front of the building on Fifth Avenue. The terrace, originally intended as an elegant forecourt for the library, suffered from some of the same problems as the park: overgrown plantings, deterioration of paving and other built elements, and appropriation by drug dealers. Hanna/Olin began with a social intent: "The terrace had to become more civic," recalls Olin. "We didn't care whether or not it was genteel, but we wanted people to be there in greater numbers and to mind their manners." (Olin would later apply the same principle to the library's "backyard.")

To cleanse the terrace of drug dealers, Olin and Arthur Rosenblatt (who was directing the project for the library), dreamed up a ruse of sorts: putting up a tall, opaque construction fence in the dealers' favorite corner of the terrace and keeping it there for two years whether construction was going forward or not. The subterfuge worked, and the dealers moved to other haunts. Meanwhile, Hanna/Olin designed new patterned paving of granite, bluestone, and cobbles which allowed more of the terrace to be used by pedestrians. They also replaced the overgrown trees and shrubs that were growing against the building with bosques of honey locusts planted further from the walls to allow clear visibility up and down the terrace. Beneath the locusts Hanna/Olin placed moveable tables and chairs where, today, library patrons read, converse, and buy snacks from food kiosks. Although the terrace overlooks Fifth Avenue and 42nd Street, the busiest corner in New York City according to a study of pedestrian traffic, it is indeed a very civic space today; drug dealers and their patrons are nowhere to be seen.

The food kiosks represent an innovative design solution in their own right. The budget would not support conventional kiosks, which would have had to conform to codes and be built by union labor. Fortunately, the architect for the kiosks, Hugh Hardy of the New York City

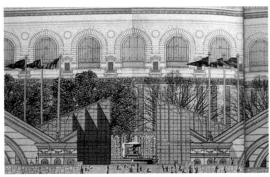

Playful scheme for a grand cafe on Sixth Avenue terrace by Hugh Hardy for Architectural League ideas exhibition

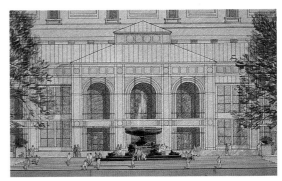

Werner LeRoy's proposal for a grand casino style cafe by Hugh Hardy with the relocated Lowell fountain

firm Hardy Holzman Pfeiffer Associates, had another idea. He had been brought on board on the basis of his flair for adding new uses to the interiors and exteriors of older buildings, and had once worked as a stage designer. Why not declare the kiosks "temporary," he suggested, and hire off-Broadway scenery shops to build them? The resulting structures were expected to last five years at most; they have now been in place since 1982, and are still functioning.

As work on the front terrace drew to a close, Olin and Hardy were asked to undertake the restoration of the library's "backyard." The Bryant Park Restoration Corporation had already entered into negotiations with the New York City Parks Department to take over management of Bryant Park; during the following year the city would effectively lease the park to the BPRC for a dollar a year, and would grant that organization responsibility for the park's redesign and management. The city would dedicate $6 million in capital funds to the park's restoration, to be matched by $3.2 million in privately-raised money.

A key innovation, to ensure ongoing funding, was the designation of a "business improvement district"—a nonprofit corporation with the power to levy assessments on all real estate surrounding the park. Charged at approximately eleven cents per square foot of office space, this assessment was to be collected by the city in the same manner as the city property tax, and immediately remitted to BPRC for maintenance and operation of the park. The amount raised in this way would be $850,000 yearly. (By 1996 it had increased to $950,000.) The Parks Department pledged $250,000 in annual support. The remainder of the $1.2 million annual budget for maintenance and operations was to come from park concessions. [12] "We were very happy to work on the park, but we quickly realized that it was a much tougher problem than the front terrace," Olin says. Because of its landmark status, he was constrained from lowering the park to street level, since that would have required cutting down the handsome plane trees. He considered ripping out the wall and fence, and surrounding the park with continuous stairs like those around a Greek temple, "but the cost of those stairs would break the bank." Many of the ideas in Olin's early design drawings ("I was having a lot of

fun," he remembers) proved equally unrealistic from a financial point of view. Hardy finally pulled him aside and said, "Laurie, you can draw really well, but we can't afford this; we don't have the budget."

Architectural design for a restaurant was going forward at the same time. In 1983, restaurateur Warner LeRoy proposed a $22 million glass-and-steel restaurant, to be designed by Hugh Hardy, on the terrace directly behind the library. The BPRC intended this to be "the financial engine that would pull this train out of the station," in Olin's words. Recalling the 1853 structure that had once existed on the site, the pavilion, with its two stories and 22-foot ceilings, was to be built against the back wall of the library. [13]

The design proposal Olin finally arrived at, shown in a rendering done in 1983, features a pair of long, narrow reflecting pools flanking the central lawn—"very French, because I see this as a very French park," says Olin. The Lowell Memorial Fountain would be put back on the terrace, where it had been sited in 1912. (It had been moved to the west end of the park with the implementation of the Lusby Simpson plan.) The William Cullen Bryant memorial would be moved to the

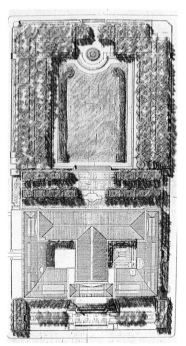

Simpson/Clark plan of 1934 as of
1980

Early abandoned Hanna/Olin Ltd.
study of civic fountain, plaza, basins
and kiosks in park with cafe

Sketch scheme for redevelopment of
park with 1000 seat cafe, Lowell
fountain restored to east terrace,
Bryant moved to Sixth Avenue
entry, basins and bridges around
the lawn

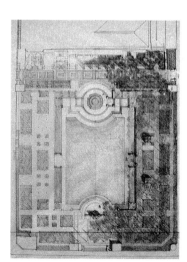

Presentation rendering of proposal
for giant cafe, and park changes
initiated in studies

Study of park by Hanna/Olin with
move of Bryant statue to Sixth
Avenue terrace, Lowell fountain
returned to the east, library terrace
enlarged and enhanced, handicap
access ramps, mid-block crossing,
opening up beneath trees, addition
of kiosks, with large single cafe on
rear terrace

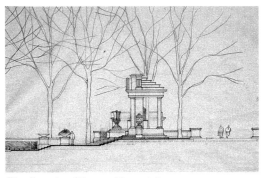

Sketch study of Bryant Memorial relocation and terrace steps from intermediate proposal

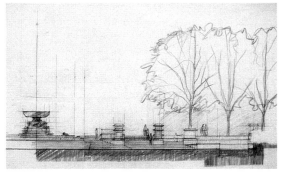

Sketch study of Lowell fountain and terrace redesign from intermediate proposal

opposite end of the park. A promenade would pass in front of the proposed restaurant, opening through-block circulation from 40th to 42nd Streets. Nevertheless, partly at the insistence of the restaurateur, who wanted to control access, the plan did not open the park as much as Whyte had recommended, or as Olin had felt to be necessary from the beginning.

"When we took this out in public a fire storm broke out," recalls Olin. The core issue was that the proposed two-story restaurant would obscure far too much of the rear facade of the beloved Carrere and Hastings building. Architectural critics charged that its architecture would be incongruous with that of the library. Many New Yorkers expressed great anxiety over the issue of the privatization of a beloved public space, however degraded the park might have become; many worried that the park might become too "gentrified." Richard Sennet, a New York University sociology professor and author of *The Fall of Public Man*, defended the right of homeless people and the drug dealers to use the park. (As it turned out, the homeless, at least, still have access to the park, as will be seen later.)

New York City Parks Commissioner Henry Stern's reaction to the proposed design was, "The circulation's too constricted. You've got to cut more openings." Olin took Stern's directive as carte blanche to break the park open. During this period, the recently published Social Life of Small Urban Spaces, with its critique of the park's access, was very much in the air, and Olin got to know Whyte and even used him as a consultant on another Hanna/Olin project. As the design for Bryant Park evolved, then, it increasingly came to reflect Whyte's recommendations.

Many community members were concerned about the planned addition of water, the moving of the fountains, and other modifications to the historic park. Some said that toddlers could drown in the pools, which, besides, would be a maintenance headache. But it was the cost estimate for the proposed design—constructing the pools and moving the existing fountain and the Bryant memorial—that finally doomed it, recalls Chris Allen, Hanna/Olin's associate in charge of the project. (Significantly, the effect of budget constraints was eventually to force a final treatment that would be more faithful to the historic design.)

Hanna/Olin was obliged to run these and other gauntlets as part of the complex public-review process, which included hearings before Community Board 5, the City Planning Commission, the Board of Estimate, the Landmarks Preservation Commission, and the Art Commission, and approval by the state legislature. Many local constituencies, like the Friends of Cast Iron, would ultimately demand input. In retrospect, Olin admits that the redesign was enriched by the public process. But he makes no bones about the tenacity Hanna/Olin needed ("We're stubborn as hell") in order to see the project through to completion in the superheated public environment.

In 1985, just when the park design seemed to be going well, Olin recalls that the library directors announced, "We may have to abandon the building. The stacks are full. We can't figure out where to expand." Olin made a suggestion: Why not put the stacks under the lawn? This would allow a relatively inexpensive, open-cut excavation, and Hanna/Olin had considerable experience in designing landscapes atop roofs and parking garages. Olin's proposal was accepted, and Davis Brody was commissioned to design the two-story stack extension, which would house 3.2 million

volumes, with a sixty-two foot long tunnel to connect it to the library building.

In 1986, after three years of negotiations, Warner LeRoy dropped his plans to build a restaurant on the terrace. Public opposition to a structure that would have obscured the rear facade of the historic library was intense. Among the groups decrying it were the Landmarks Commission, the Municipal Arts Society, the Parks Council, and the *New York Times*. LeRoy refused to scale down; instead, he pulled out. This left the BPRC without the food service on which its entire financial strategy depended. The following year the BPRC proposed two one-story restaurants on the upper terrace, and four kiosks in the park, all to be designed by Hugh Hardy. Ultimately, on June 15, 1988, the New York City Art Commission approved the design for both restaurants and kiosks and, on July 11, the design for the park itself. The Parks Council praised the design, as did the Municipal Art Society and the Fine Arts Federation. With a chain-link fence to secure the area, Bryant Park then became a construction site, as contractors excavated a 35-foot-deep hole where the lawn had been, to house the new stacks designed by Davis Brody. Simultaneously, a group of private

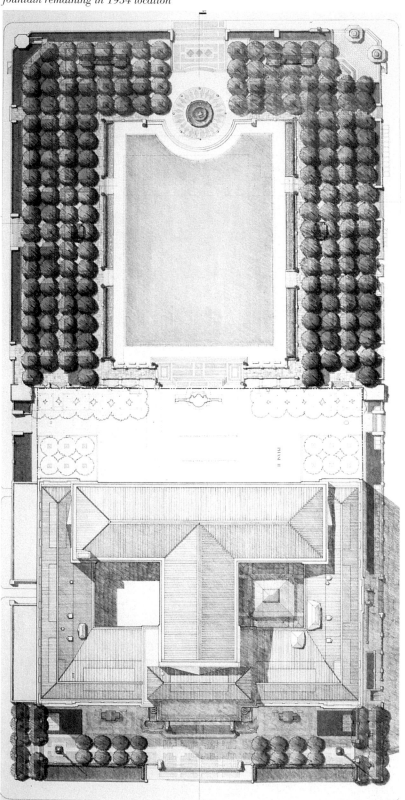

*Approved scheme for twin one-story
garden pavilion, cafes*

*Hanna/Olin Ltd. early drawing of
flower borders*

Olin watercolor of 42nd Street library entry with addition of handicap ramp

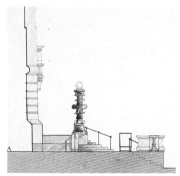

Section of revised 42nd Street entry stair with handicap access ramp

New mold for re-casting Carrere and Hastings torcheres

security officers began a neighborhood sweep aimed at clearing the park and the surrounding business improvement district of drug dealers and other lawbreakers. [14]

Hanna/Olin's role in the park's reconstruction required painstaking attention to such details as the dismantling, cleaning, and general restoration of most existing park elements—railings and monuments, for example. Where possible, the original bluestone was reset. The fountain received new mechanical systems. "We threw out very little," says Olin. "We essentially mined the site." There was one element, however, that Whyte, in his original recommendations, had suggested jettisoning: the iron perimeter fence. Here the Friends of Cast Iron, advocates for the preservation of iron architectural details in New York, reared their collective head at public hearings. At their insistence the fence was dismantled, repaired, and repainted—and it stayed. Where the plan had to be changed to improve circulation or for other reasons, Hanna/Olin strove to replicate the original design intent as closely as possible. From the archives of the Parks Department, the staff obtained the original Moses-era drawings of construction details; they field-verified the

dimensions of these details by photographing and measuring all site elements. This research was critical. For example, in order to make new entrances, the perimeter railing had to be pierced and new end posts introduced along the stairs; Hanna/Olin designed new end posts, following the original drawings. Even where entire new elements were added—the ramps to the upper terrace for the handicapped, for example—they were designed and executed in the manner of the original work. Only twelve of the plane trees, planted in 1934, were taken from the park in the reconfiguration of the space. Six trees that were dead or dying were replaced.

Overall, says Olin, "absolute attention was paid to historic details, not so much in terms of where the elements were (we moved some around) but, where we had to introduce new elements, we respected the original materials and design. The modifications were made to introduce new life into the park." One such modification was the considerable enlargement of the central lawn "to create a generous space with the sun streaming in," says Olin. "I see the lawn as a symbol of tranquility in this setting; I wanted it to be as

New handicap access ramps to rear terrace from lawn area during construction

Site demolition, Sixth Avenue entry to park for reconfiguration of stair

generous and full as possible—a big, soft, green, velvety carpet that would offer a dramatic alternative to the often dark, obdurate canyons of Manhattan."

Given such changes, does Bryant Park deserve the historic-restoration label? "I don't think there's such a thing as landscape restoration," declares Olin. "If there were, it would be a form of taxidermy. Time goes in one direction; so do landscapes. To restore this park would have been to produce a social sink. Anyway, what period would you restore it to—the 1920s or the 1940s? The important thing was to figure out how to open it up so that no one felt trapped."

In 1989, the new library stacks were roofed over, covered with insulation and drainage material, with a final layer of topsoil—parks commissioner Henry Stern insisted on a generous six feet of soil on the premise that future generations might want to plant trees—and seeded. One problem was the intrusion of vents and stairwells from the underground stacks into the lawn and adjacent planting beds. Minimizing their impact on the historic park became, Olin remembers, "an ongoing battle." Today, a visitor is not at all

aware that there are 84 miles of shelving underneath the lawn. The one trapdoor that serves as an emergency exit from the stacks into the park lies camouflaged beneath a commemorative plaque. The subterranean infrastructure of the city also affected the construction process. When the contractor was building the new 42nd Street entrance, "All of a sudden the sidewalk gave way and there was the fan room for the subway!" Olin recalls. Construction came to a halt until the damage was repaired. Less serious was the unearthing of an old water main while excavating for a drainage line—a reminder of the network of pipes under the park, some of which dated back to the time of the Croton Reservoir.

The restoration of Bryant Park was more likely to attract private donations than were improvements to other public parks because of its high public profile and the importance of the site. In 1989, library chairman Heiskell opened a fund-raising campaign with a press reception and walking tour of the fenced construction site. The campaign yielded $2 million in gifts from Enid Haupt; from the Swig, Weiler, and Arnow families; from Arthur

Excavation for new library stacks under construction

Underground library stacks under construction

Installation of soil, curbs, walks, and irrigation over library stacks

One level of library stacks prior to installation of moveable compact shelving and books

Parks Commissioner Elizabeth Gottbaum, Councilwoman Carol Greiter, and Governor Mario Cuomo, and Mayor David Dinkins at reopening ceremonies

Mr. and Mrs. William H. Whyte at reopening ceremonies

Ross; and from the Rockefeller Brothers Fund. To a BPRC request for $50,000 for the restoration of the William Cullen Bryant Memorial, the J.M. Kaplan Fund responded with a proposal of its own. "Much as we love and respect Mr. Bryant and good public art," said fund president Joan Davidson, "We decided public comfort facilities were essential to life in the city and told BPRC we would prefer to fix up the park's public restrooms."

Because of the cost of the park's restoration—the price tag for the entire operation was to be $8.9 million—the BPRC was continually searching for funds. ("We were all out with our begging bowls," recalls Olin.) The 1,100 moveable chairs specified by Hanna/Olin, for example, were obtained at a discount through one of Arthur Rosenblatt's connections. And premier garden designer Lynden Miller, brought on board to design the plantings for the 300-foot-long perennial beds which Hanna/Olin had designed to border the great lawn, solicited donations from her Manhattan social circle.

By late 1991 the restoration was nearing completion, and that fall Miller led a team in planting 2,000 perennials in the planting beds. The resulting floral displays provide, says Olin, "all the joy and seasonal richness that people expect from public gardens." Indeed, a burst of spring bulbs the following April heralded the opening of the new Bryant Park, and Holly Whyte, old and infirm but smiling broadly, attended the opening ceremonies. Hanna/Olin, after all, had given built form to every one of his 1979 recommendations, save that of removing the perimeter fence. More importantly, the spirit of his vision for the park had been fulfilled.

The public wasted no time in filling the 1,100 moveable chairs, and scheduled entertainment was initiated with a series of 60 free concerts and a weekly "Comedy in the Park" series. And the drug dealers? Finding not only a round-the-clock police presence but an absence of dark corners, they went looking for other haunts. "Bad people need darkness to do nefarious acts. They just don't like to do them in public," says library director Marshall Rose. "The biggest problem since the restoration," he says, "is that some people are sitting in the flower beds during Monday night films. That's a bigger problem than crime."

Summer jazz festival on lawn

The sound of laughing children is a welcome addition to Bryant Park

Bryant Park Today: "A Monument of Genuine Joy"

To a visitor today, Bryant Park seems the most vibrant, welcoming outdoor space in midtown Manhattan. The first impression is of a light-filled space in the midst of midtown's daunting density, a space that is easy to enter and easy to leave—and to see into. That this impression is shared by most park users was confirmed by a post-occupancy evaluation, performed between March 30 and August 24, 1993, by City University of New York (CUNY) graduate students. The study used behavioral mapping and open-ended interviews to uncover the feelings and reactions of users of the park to its redesign and new management.

To some extent, the study results confirmed the obvious—that perceived safety is the primary reason for the park's new popularity ("Before the renovation, I wouldn't even walk past the park," said one respondent). The study also confirmed the fact that design for greater visual and physical access to the park has been critical to its increasing use. [16] The presence of police officers, security guards, and park maintenance workers

Lunch hour music concert

Moveable chairs provide seating area on lawn

Moveable chairs in gravel have replaced ivy beds

Mid-day relaxation

was also cited as critical to perceived safety. (The park maintains a full-time staff of about 35 people, including a full-time horticulturist, a maintenance and sanitation crew, and a security team that operates twenty-four hours a day, seven days a week.[16] Olin makes no bones about the role of maintenance and operations (security, for example) in the ongoing success of the park. "I now know that design alone can't rehabilitate a landscape," he says. "You have to have good management.")

Respondents in the CUNY study also cited the availability and flexibility of seating as prime reasons for visiting the park. Locating a bench, or a ledge, or a folding chair is apparently quite easy, except during the crowded lunchtime period, when such ancillary seating areas as the ledge along the lawn and the curving steps receive their heaviest use. The number of the French-made folding chairs is now up to 2,000. "I don't think there's a place in the United States with as many moveable chairs," says BPRC director Daniel Biederman.

In reflecting on the park's extraordinary success as a magnet for users Olin reflects: "We're sort of humble about the part we played. As designers we can provide the armature, but we can't make people use the space." He adds, however, that "New Yorkers don't need an operating manual on how to use an urban space." The depressed central lawn, surrounded by the inhabited edge under the plane trees appeals, he believes, to New Yorkers' sense of theater. He recalls observing the users on a sunny day: "Up until about 11:00 A.M. people watch the lawn. Then someone tests the waters—and it's everyone into the pool. The lawn is crowded from then on."

Not mentioned in the CUNY study, but apparent to any visitor, is the extraordinary diversity of park users—from young executives to the elderly and from fashionable jet-setters to families pushing their young children in strollers. Most surprising of all, perhaps, is that a scattering of homeless people are still in evidence in this elegantly appointed park, sitting quietly, with their belongings in makeshift vehicles beside them. Even more surprising, the mainstream users, who greatly outnumber the homeless, seem to tolerate their presence. Of course, they must obey the clearly posted (and enforced) park regulations. No alcohol. No panhandling. No rummaging in trash cans. If they fol-low the rules, however, they are accepted. "We don't take action against people because of their social status—only because of behavior," says the BPRC's Andrew Manshell. Homeless people (or anyone else) may even sleep on the lawn whenever the park is open (provided, says Manshell, that they do not attempt to sleep on cardboard, which harms the turf).

Fears that the park would become "gentrified" as a result of privatization have apparently proved groundless. Paul Goldberger confirmed what is obvious to most users. "In practical terms, [privatization] has yielded only good results. Under the corporation's enlightened supervision, the park has become a more truly public place than at any time in the last generation."[17]

To anyone familiar with the stresses of life in New York City, the relaxed, convivial mood of park users is remarkable. Particularly sociable is the crowd around the chess tables near Sixth Avenue, where a nearby chess-supply store rents out equipment, and onlookers stand close to view interesting matches. Although critics of privatization might protest that this is another example of commercialization (BPRC does receive a share of the pro-ceeds), Bryant Park is fast replacing Washington Square Park as the city's chess mecca.

Park attendance is up considerably from the low lunchtime attendance of only 700 recorded in 1980. The park supervisor keeps a regular tally of total attendance. On a typical weekday in September 1995 he recorded 1,401 people in the park at 12:40 P.M. and 2,079 at 1:40 P.M. Significantly, the average ratio of female visitors for those two hours was 43.6 per cent—about double the 1980 figure.[18] "One of the things I'm most proud of in this park," says Olin, "is that a woman can take off her shoes and fall asleep without worrying about who's sitting next to her." Particularly astonishing, in a city where a clean, functioning outdoor public restroom is almost unheard of, is the condition of the restored public restrooms. The Carrere and Hastings pavilion adjacent to 42nd Street, originally the men's restroom, has been meticulously fitted out with both men's and ladies' rooms, and a full-time attendant keeps the facilities gleaming while hurrying loiterers along. (If, for example, a homeless person attempts to take a sponge bath in the sink, he is immediately

New, open, broad stairs from Sixth Avenue to the park

The sale of park benches has been a successful fund-raising approach to help with the cost of park maintenance

New torchere at mid-block entry

advised—diplomatically—that there are other people waiting in line.) The pavilion at the other end of the terrace has been restored as a park office.

Bryant Park has won a host of honors, from high-profile national awards—an Honor Award for Urban Design from the American Institute of Architects, an Outstanding Planning Award from the American Planning Association, the Star Award from the Regional Plan Association, and a Merit Award from the American Society of Landscape Architects—to such humble kudos as the East Side Association's Green Thumb Award.

Newspaper and magazine articles have been almost exclusively rave reviews; Time magazine named Bryant Park the "Best Design of 1992." New York magazine called it "a touch of the Tuileries . . . the perfect endorsement for restoring public spaces with private funds."[19] The most insightful of the many *New York Times* articles was by Paul Goldberger, who called the restored park "a monument of genuine joy." He added, "At first glance, the park looks almost the same, just a cleaner and fresher version of the old . . . but the cumulative effect of small changes is to render it a dramatically

different place, vastly more open than before, more tied to the street and the city around it. . . . Small changes in an unworkable design fixed what was broken."[20]

Like all nonprofit institutions, the Bryant Park Restoration Corporation is continually seeking sources of additional funding—particularly since the New York Parks Department, which had originally pledged to increase its annual contribution to the park's upkeep over time, in fact reduced that contribution, in 1996, from $250,000 to $200,000. The BPRC would like to expand its services—keeping the park open until 1:00 A.M. winter and summer, renovating the pavilion at the corner of 40th and Sixth Avenue (the last-needed capital improvement), and instituting a sculpture program. These would require increasing the current $1.2 million operating budget to $2 million. The BPRC has used the park in various ways in order to generate revenue. As an example, for the past three years some of the most prestigious fashion shows in the country have taken place in tents set up on the lawn, in both spring and fall. Another fund-raising approach has been the sale of park benches emblazoned with

the name of the purchaser. (Wood-and-wrought-iron models fetch $5,000, concrete versions $10,000; such celebrities as Yoko Ono and Martha Stewart are already represented.) Olin takes a long view of any fluctuations in the park's cash flow. "The park now has a constituency of tens of thousands of people," he says. "It's going to endure."

In his book *City*, Holly Whyte has offered his most recent comment on the Hanna/Olin design, writing that it "looks very much like the old one but in function is the opposite of it."[21] Olin agrees, but prefers to describe Bryant Park with a quotation from Dwight D. Eisenhower: "Things are more the way they used to be than they have ever been before." He continues, "I've done projects that set out to be modernist works. This was a project that set out to save a space in the public realm. It had nothing to do with style and very little to do with personality, except the ability to hang in there and stay flexible as the situation evolved and changed. . . . A lot of what we did was sleight of hand—the nuances in this park are quite subtle. Mies was right: God is in the details."

Bryant Park:
Photographs and Drawings

1   Bryant sculpture
2   Lawn
3   Fountain
4   Perennial border
5   Gravel walk
6   Ramp
7   Vending kiosk
8   Original main entrance
9   Expanded Entrance
10 New entrance
11 Information kiosk
12 Restrooms
13 Restaurant

SIXTH AVENUE

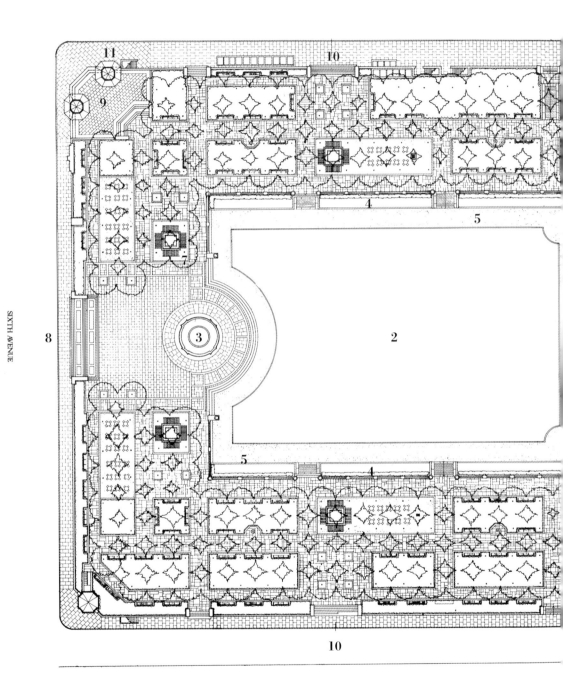

0 ———— 64 feet

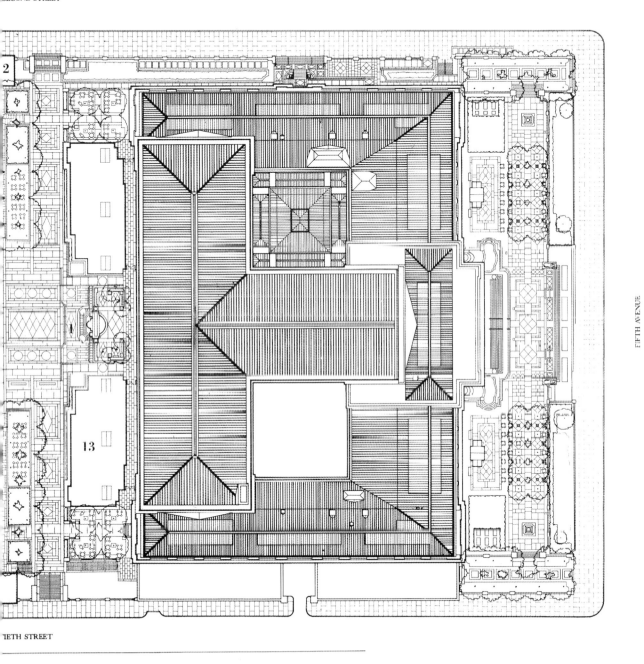

SECOND STREET

FIFTH AVENUE

IETH STREET

Final plan of Bryant Park

FORTY SECOND STREET

Stacks Level 2

Stacks Level 1

0 _____ 64 feet

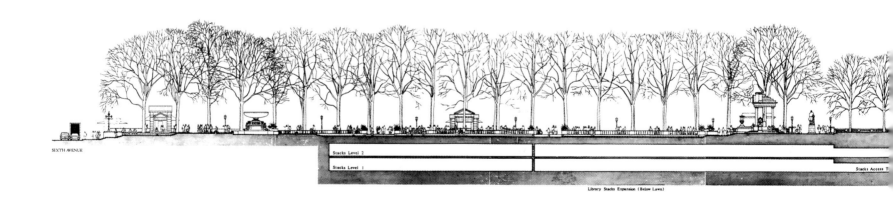

SIXTH AVENUE

Stacks Level 2

Stacks Level 1

Stacks Access T

Library Stacks Expansion (Below Lawn)

0 _____ 64 feet

FORTIETH STREET

xpansion (Below Lawn)

*North-South cross section of park indicating
underground stacks of library beneath the
lawn (Olin Partnership)*

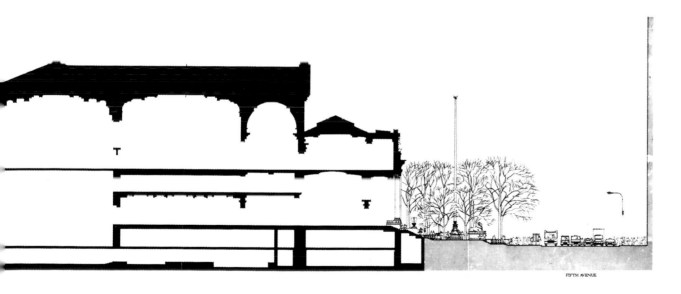

FIFTH AVENUE

*East-West cross section of park with stacks
(Olin Partnership)*

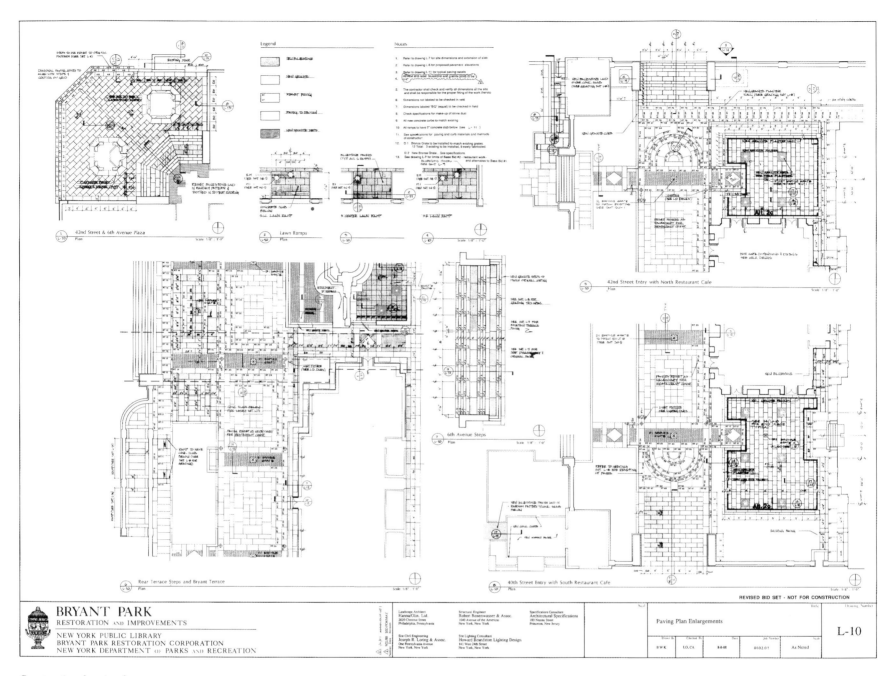

BRYANT PARK
RESTORATION AND IMPROVEMENTS

NEW YORK PUBLIC LIBRARY
BRYANT PARK RESTORATION CORPORATION
NEW YORK DEPARTMENT OF PARKS AND RECREATION

Paving Plan Enlargements

L-10

REVISED BID SET - NOT FOR CONSTRUCTION

*Construction drawing for pavement
and kiosk layout and installation
(Olin Partnership)*

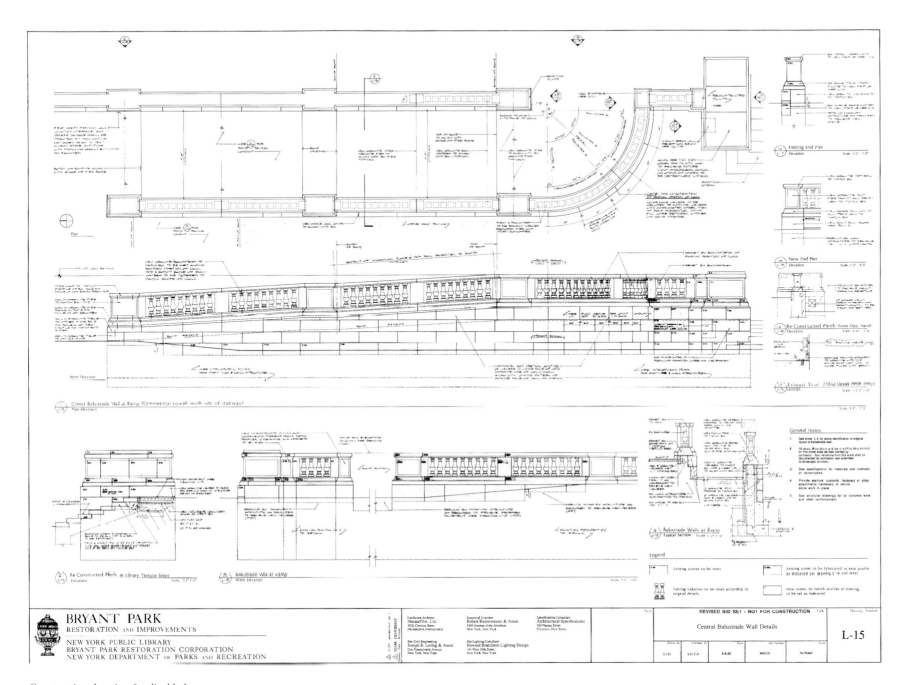

BRYANT PARK
RESTORATION AND IMPROVEMENTS

NEW YORK PUBLIC LIBRARY
BRYANT PARK RESTORATION CORPORATION
NEW YORK DEPARTMENT OF PARKS AND RECREATION

Central Balustrade Wall Details

L-15

*Construction drawing for disabled access
ramp, railings, and stair (Olin Partnership)*

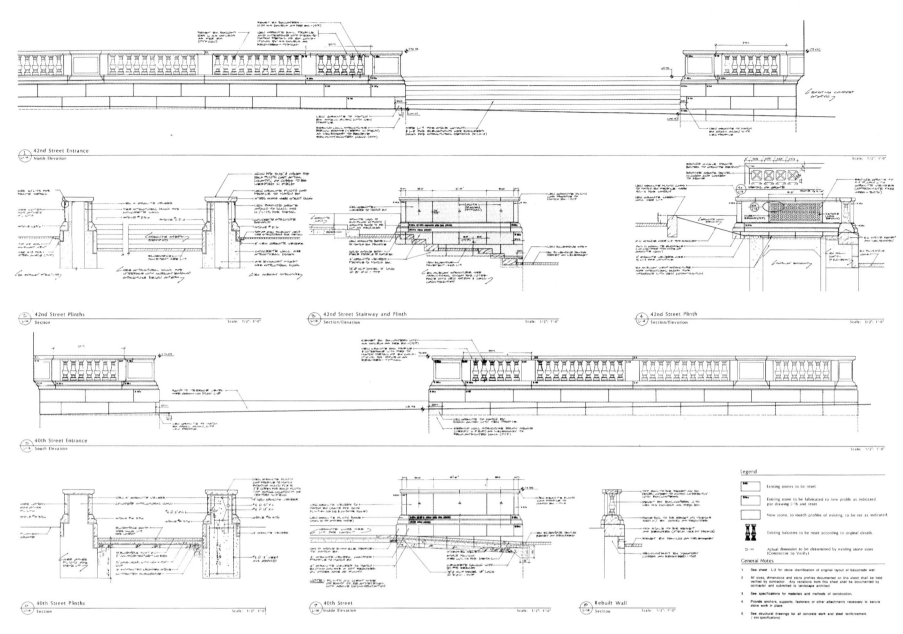

Construction drawings for new openings, stairs, and access in existing walls and railings (Olin Partnership)

Notes

1. Claudia Deutsch, "Once Anathema, Now a Midtown Marketing Tool," *New York Times*, 6 (June 1993).

2. Frederick R. Steiner and Todd Johnson, "Perfecting the Ordinary," *Landscape Architecture*, (March 1992), 70.

3. Stephen Carr et al, *Public Space* (Cambridge, England: Cambridge University Press,1992), 165.

4. William H. Whyte, *The Social Life of Small Urban Spaces* (Washington, D. C.: The Conservation Foundation, 1980), 58.

5. The *New York Times*, 23 January 1928, quoted in "Project for Public Spaces—Bryant Park: Intimidation or Recreation?" (report to the Rockefeller Foundation, 1981), 6.

6. Project for Public Spaces, 7.

7. Project for Public Spaces, 15-19.

8. William H. Whyte, "Revitalization of Bryant Park" 9 (report to the Rockefeller Brothers Fund, 26 November 1979), 1.

9. Paul Goldberger, "Bryant Park, An Out of Town Experience," *New York Times*, May 3, 1992, Section 2, 34.

10. Whyte, Revitalization of Bryant Park, 6.

11. Daniel Biederman and A.R. Nager, "Up From Smoke. A New Improved Bryant Park?" *New York Affairs*, 6 (1981): 104.

12. Andrew Manshell, "Bryant Park: A Model for the Future," *The Public Garden* (January 1993): 13.

13. Deirdre Carmody, "Vast Rebuilding of Bryant Park Planned," *New York Times*, 1 (December 1983), sec. B2.

14. "Milestones in the Greening of Bryant Park," *Bryant Park News*, (Fall/Winter 1994), 3.

15. Sukwon Park, "Post-occupancy Evaluation of Bryant Park" (paper for 1993 CUNY graduate class in environmental psychology), 25.

16. "A Day in the Life of Bryant Park," *Bryant Park News*, Fall/Winter 1995, 2.

17. Goldberger, 34.

18. "A Day in the Life of Bryant Park," 3.

19. "The Best of New York," *New York* (December 20-27, 1993), 27.

20. Goldberger, 34.

21. William H. Whyte, *City: Rediscovering the Center* (New York: Doubleday, 1988), 160.

Photography Credits